Mothers, Your Best *Is* Good Enough

LUCILE JOHNSON

Compiled and Edited by Arlene Bascom

Covenant Communications, Inc.

Published by Covenant Communications, Inc.
American Fork, Utah

Copyright © 1994 by Lucile Johnson
All rights reserved
Printed in the United States of America
First printing: April 1994

99 98 97 96 95 94   10 9 8 7 6 5 4 3

ISBN 1-55503-554-X

A young mother arose to bear her testimony and said, "I want to be the *best* mother all the time, but I'm not. I'm only a good mother *sometimes*." She began to weep and sat down.

In my experience, most mothers feel exactly as she did. I do not personally know one solitary mother who thinks she has done a great job as a mother and is totally satisfied with her job performance.

I have heard some men extol their angel mothers in the same way Abe Lincoln did and describe a mother who never raised her voice, lost her cool, or was ever, ever angry. However, I'm sure these "angel" mothers rarely felt like angels, and I am also sure the men recalling their mothers have memories more nostalgic than accurate!

Still, most mothers are more angel than they dream. It isn't because they don't ever get impatient or angry or raise their voices or nag, but maybe *because* of it . . . those things often show how *much* they care.

In 1979, a tough-acting juvenile was brought into the probation offices where I was counseling. He swaggered in and acted like a really tough kid. Juvenile offenders are allowed one phone call. When I asked whom he would like to call and suggested that perhaps he would want to call his dad, he emphatically said, "No. I want to call my mother."

The boy broke down in tears on the phone and sobbed his heart out, "Mom, I want to come home!"

Because he was a member of the Church, I decided to talk with the boy privately until his mother came. He said, "I will never do this dumb thing again. I can't

believe I could hurt my mom so much. She doesn't deserve it."

"What about your dad?" I asked.

"Oh, Dad's never around. He's so busy and involved, he doesn't know what's going on in the family, and I really don't think he cares. But Mom does. Oh, she yells a lot. She nags and she's always on my back, but I'll tell you one thing. She cares! She really cares about me and what happens to me and that means a lot. Do you know what she said on the phone? She asked *me* to forgive *her*. She was sorry she had failed me somehow. I was supposed to *forgive* her? Forgive her for what? For being a mother who loved me when I don't even deserve it?"

Mothers, don't beat yourself with guilt and regrets because you "yelled a lot" or "nagged a lot." Many mothers seem to wear guilt like an old bathrobe that is too familiar to discard. So, you yelled and nagged. Is there a mother alive who hasn't done both? But did you love those children? Did they, and do they, know you love them? That is what really counts.

Granted, motherhood is a demanding, frustrating, often thankless task, as the husband of one of my clients learned first hand. I'll call him Ken and his wife Joanne.

Ken was a very successful young entrepreneur. Ken and Joanne had five children, three of them pre-schoolers. When Ken would come home at night, he was not very pleased with the way Joanne kept the house. As a matter of fact, he thought she was a pretty poor excuse for a housekeeper. The first thing he would say almost without fail when he came home was, "What have you been doing all day?"

One day when he came in and there were lots of toys and clutter strewn around, Ken said, "What is your problem? Why can't you keep this stuff picked up?" Joanne looked at him tearfully as he continued, "Let me tell you, Joanne, what your problem is. Your problem is lack of organization. Everything in life can be handled by the principle of organization. If I ran my office the way you run this house, we would be bankrupt." To add insult to injury he added, "By the way, I have a secretary who is great at organization. I ought to bring her in here. She could teach you some things."

Joanne was simply cut to the quick, but the next morning she had a plan. The next day when Ken went to work and the older children went to school, she told the three younger children they were going to have a little vacation. They could stay in their nightclothes if they wanted to, and they could do as they pleased all day.

They had an absolutely marvelous time! Joanne read magazines and ate snacks, and the children ate graham crackers in the living room, spread their toys all over, and had quite a day. The mess from food preparation was not cleaned up. Everything was left right where it was used. Not a single dish was washed, not a floor was swept or mopped, not a bathroom taken care of, not a bed made.

When Ken came home and saw this mess, he nearly exploded. *"What have you been doing all day?"* he raged, but this time Joanne was ready for that question.

"Absolutely nothing! Absolutely nothing of what I do every day, and this is what would happen if I didn't do *every day* all the things you don't give me one bit of credit for."

But Ken wasn't convinced and he replied, "I want to tell you something, Joanne. I could run this house

smooth as silk, with one hand tied behind my back." This gave Joanne an idea.

She said, "All right! Let's just trade roles for a little while, and I won't even require that you have your hands tied behind your back. You know, I've had business training. I'll get up in the morning and run your office for a week, and you stay here and run the house."

Ken laughed. "Great! I need a vacation!" And together they set out the stipulations of the things he would have to do at home and the things she would do at the office.

Joanne told me later, "I just couldn't wait. Imagine being able to get up in the morning and get dressed up and get your hair all done and leave that tacky house and all of those kids, and get to go to a nice clean office and eat lunch at McDonald's every day!"

Ken added, "I was excited. This would be such a wonderful object lesson for Joanne. I was going to prove to her that the name of the game was "organization," and besides, I was planning all these extra things to do with all the blocks of time I could create."

At the end of the week, Ken's words had significantly changed. They were so poignant, I wrote them down.

He said, " I battled constantly with sticky fingers, dirty noses, dirty bottoms, quarrels, and spills. My clean windows were soon smudged, my freshly mopped floors soon dirty. There was jelly on the refrigerator, peanut butter on the chairs, there was even ice cream on my new stereo! One day when the children were particularly quarrelsome and uncooperative, to my horror I heard myself saying, 'You just wait till your mother comes home!' I knew the time

had come to take off my apron and to welcome back my dearly beloved genius of a wife and mother and homemaker."

Well, you can imagine that Ken never again asked Joanne what she had been doing all day. In fact, in his repentance process, he penned some words so beautiful that a national magazine published them.

"There is no job in all of the world more overwhelming, more taxing, more relentless, more frustrating, and more thankless than that of a wife and a mother and a homemaker. To realize that it is done so well by so many who know and appreciate their awesome responsibilities is the greatest tribute that could ever be paid to another human being." And I say *amen!*

Let me tell you about another angel mother I became acquainted with through her son, who told me his story.

Lt. Col. Chaplain Claude Newby, U.S. Army, a convert to the Church, is a highly decorated combat chaplain. He was raised in the hills of Tennessee. His family was certainly "poverty level." Claude was held back in grade school for two years because the school regarded him as retarded and unable to learn. However, Claude's mother defended "her boy." Every time the school suggested Claude was too slow for public school, she responded, "You don't see the light in his eyes because you won't take the time to *look*."

Whatever his heartache or humiliation, Claude's mother would say simply, "Son, I believe in you."

When Claude was in the seventh grade, a near riot broke out on the school bus. The huge bus driver stopped the bus, and threatened, "If there is one more

word spoken, that student will be expelled from school." The bus was deadly quiet until the bus began to move again. Then, despite the warning, a student sitting next to Claude began to talk. Claude had not uttered a word. The bus driver accused Claude of talking, and amidst the jeers of the other students, put him bodily off the bus, saying he could not return to school unless his father personally brought him to the principal.

At home that night, when Claude told his story, his mother stood up and said, "I believe you, son." The next day his mountaineer father, grim-lipped, took him back to school. The principal heard Claude's story and said quietly but with conviction, "I believe you, Claude Newby."

Though she was old beyond her years, worn and tired from her tasks as a mother of many children, though she had no education and no personal opportunities, she took the time to see the light in her boy's eyes when others saw him only as slow.

This mother, who had never been to school, said, "I believe in you," and when a judgment was to be made she said, "I believe *you.*"

The event the students looked forward to the most each school year came when a bus was chartered to go to a distant town for a ball game. For one such occasion, Claude worked hard and collected enough whiskey bottles to sell to a mooshiner for the necessary one dollar bus fare. Before the trip, the principal came to Claude's class to take a head count of those students who would be going. He passed up and down each row, but when he came to Claude's desk he said, "No use asking—I know you aren't going." Claude was too humiliated to correct him.

Claude Newby, whom the school had seen as

retarded, went on to receive advanced degrees and encouraged others to do the same. While in the service, he saved lives and affected many positively. Who can estimate his personal impact in a thirty-year military career?

How and why did this happen? Because he had a mother, who, although she could neither read nor write, *loved* him and *believed* in him. When a mother can do that, it matters little what else she can or cannot do.

I spoke to a woman in a neighboring state recently about the death of her mother. Annie had never had a very good relationship with her mother because, as she explained, "My mother was always critical of me, and always saying things that hurt me."

When Annie knew her mother was in the hospital dying, she did not really want to go to her, but she knew she must. After she arrived at the hospital to see her mother, she found that nothing had changed. It was just as it had always been. Each time she visited her mother, Annie steeled herself for the hurtful comments her mother might make to her, and she found herself dreading the visits, yet feeling guilty for not wanting to be there.

One day at the hospital, a Polynesian girl was cleaning the room while Annie and her mother were having one of their "conversations." As Annie and the girl were both leaving, the girl said, "I begrudge you the mother talk." Annie asked her what she meant, and she said, "My mother died when I was 12 years old, and I don't have no one to give me that *mother* talk."

Annie told me, "Instinctively, I knew what she was saying. My mother was like a mother bear. A mother

bear would give her life for her cubs, but she cuffs them. My mother was just cuffing me, and this girl was missing her mother's cuffing."

Once Annie understood that her mother was doing what she was doing because she cared and wanted to be a good mother, she was able to forgive her mother for hurting her. They enjoyed the most wonderful two weeks of their lives together before her mother died.

Very often I have distraught mothers say to me, "Oh Lucile, I've made such mistakes in my role as a mother." I remember one sweet stake Relief Society president who wanted to talk with me. She was the mother of five grown children who were married in the temple, sons who had been on missions, etc. She was a remarkably successful woman, as far as I could tell. Yet she shared with me, with some pathos, that she and her husband had been taking a class on marriage and parenting and that she was so depressed because she had made every mistake in the book... every mistake! She said, "Obviously, I'm a lousy mother. There are so many things I've done wrong."

I had to kind of smile and I went back over the information about her children who seemed to be very outstanding, well functioning human beings, but she persisted. "But, Lucile, really..." And then she went on to explain some of the things the class had made her realize: "I should have done this, and I shouldn't have done that. I should have said this, and I didn't say that, and... the class just keeps pointing out all the errors I've made."

I talked to her about how hard we are on ourselves as mothers. We read articles and attend classes, and we are apprised of the things we should be doing and

the things that we shouldn't be doing. And, of course, up against such ideal pictures of parenting, most of us fall short!

I said, "Of course you made mistakes and will continue to make them, but remember you did the best you could in the past with what you knew at the time, and you are still doing the best you can. God himself will not ask more of you than that."

I want to share with you, as I shared with her, that being a good mother is just making more right decisions than wrong decisions, and that you should be a little kinder to yourself, a little more generous to yourself. And how about being a nurturing parent to yourself too?

Our middle son was eight years old when we lived in Maryland at a military post. My husband felt he was lucky to be the branch president where every sister was so gifted. Each had wonderful homemaking, mothering, and teaching skills. It seemed they had it all.

I felt very inferior, especially to the sister who lived next door because she was a wonderful cook, and that was not my strong point. This sister baked bread and pies and cakes that were truly awesome. One summer evening, my eight-year-old Bart and the next-door neighbor's daughter were talking on our back porch and I overheard Nancy say, "I bet you wish you had my mother instead of yours. She made us the best supper." And Nancy began a recitation of delectable food they had just consumed. I could just imagine Bart's mouth watering, for I knew mine was. Then Nancy asked, "What did *you* have for supper, Bart?"

There was a silence and then dear, loyal little Bart, who couldn't recall a single delicious dish, said, "Well, my mother is very nice." How I cringed! I worried too.

Would Bart grow up scarred because he had no memories of hot baked bread or lemon pie?

The next day when I was taking Bart to Primary, I said, "Bart, when you grow up, what will you remember about me?" During the silence I thought accusingly to myself, "Just as I suspected. Bart is growing up scarred and wounded. What a terrible mother I am!"

Then Bart snuggled over close to me and said, "Mother, I will remember you always smelled so good."

I was surprised and pleased. As the miles rolled by I thought, "Maybe, just maybe, that is almost as good as remembering the smell of freshly baked bread." I realized that my little son was really saying he had spent a lot of pleasant moments being close to me!

Go ahead. Buy perfume, bath powder, and bubble bath for yourself and use them—you deserve a little pampering. But remember that at the same time, you are giving your little ones all the reasons you can give them to want to be close to you. You never know when you will make a memory that will linger for years.

Women are nurturers to their children, to their companions, and to everyone else—even their own mothers, and their mothers-in-law, and their neighbors. But they are often at the bottom of the totem pole when it comes to *being* nurtured. Too often they forget to nurture themselves. They don't know how to ask for what they need from others, and they don't know how to give themselves credit for what they do right.

In a fast and testimony meeting in Lethbridge, Canada, a young mother tearfully confessed, "I have overdosed on drugs and I have been suicidal. My depression has been so black, not because I lost a home in a mud slide, like some of you have, but because of little things—like my little girl wasn't potty

trained, my husband wasn't affectionate, my older son was rude, or the weeds were taking over the garden and five pepper plants died."

Self-pity and depression are often the results of inappropriate guilt—one of the primary sins of mothers. It was the bottom line in this mother's problem. She unconsciously felt she *should* be able to have her daughter potty trained, she *should* be able to get her husband to be more affectionate, she *should* be able to teach her son not to be rude, and she *should* be able to keep the garden weeded. When she could not control everything around her, she felt guilty and incompetent when she was actually doing the best she could.

One way to conquer inappropriate guilt is to make friends with a pad of paper. Whenever you feel distressed, overwhelmed, depressed, or angry, write down your feelings using free-flowing handwriting and descriptive language such as: "I feel angry. Why do I feel angry? I am depressed and lonely. Why do I feel like this?" Pull out all the data you have in your computer brain and write about it. Be expressive, be dramatic. Ignoring or denying feelings won't diminish them, but writing them down often will. Putting our feelings into words often helps us sort them out and get rid of the inappropriate ones.

Counselors call this type of writing "emotional vomiting," and it is very healing. It gets negative feelings out of your system and cleanses the body and mind. However, you may want to scribble over each line to make the words unreadable or tear the paper into bits and throw it away after you have finished writing. You want to get the feelings out, not recycle them by reading them over. Women are naturally gifted as healers. Use some healing on

yourself—you deserve it, and you will be a better mother because of it.

You should recognize that for the most part you are undoubtedly a very good mother indeed. Do not feel that the so-called child care authorities are privy to some kind of inspiration or knowledge that is kept from you. That is not true. What I could give you as a rule of thumb is this: Compare what you hear from "experts," or what you read in books, to the gospel of Jesus Christ. If the information does not conform, then you have absolute authority to forget it because it is simply someone's opinion, and it will not survive!

You were sent here into your mothering role and given the awesome responsibility for the physical, emotional, and spiritual welfare of your children without any experience or expertise. Why do you suppose that Heavenly Father has so decreed that we become parents without any previous experience? I think it is because he wants us to be on our knees where we need to be, seeking him, pleading for patience and forbearance and understanding.

In missionary work, what is the first thing an investigator is asked to do without fail? *Pray!* Sixty-three of my counseling clients who admitted to a diminished testimony listed faith as the number one reason: "I didn't want to pray."

A major area where Satan will work on you is to beguile and persuade you to let your prayers slip, and then let them go completely. When the regularity of your prayers decreases, your spirituality begins to diminish. As mothers, we cannot afford to let our prayers slip. When you pray regularly and sincerely, your heart will not be troubled. You will not be afraid, and you will have peace of mind.

I remember a woman in Napa, California, who came up to visit with me after one of my talks, and she told me she had nine children. I asked her how she kept her balance with that much responsibility, and she replied, "I just mop and pray, and wash and pray, and clean and pray, and cook and pray!"

One of my clients, a convert to the Church, is a student at BYU. In speaking of his background, he said, "I came from a home of poverty—such unbelievable poverty you cannot imagine."

I nodded compassionately, picturing some kind of a tenement house in California. Then, to my surprise he said, "Our home cost $250,000, and our cars were Lincolns or Cadillacs. My mother always had a maid. I went to private schools. We vacationed in Hawaii or the Caribbean. My father is a prominent doctor."

Then he continued, "But I had never prayed in my life until I was a grown man and the missionaries taught me how. Prayers were never a part of my home life. So you see how I came from a home of poverty? My life totally changed when I learned how to pray!"

Mothers, you may not live in a home of affluence, with maids to do the dirty work. Perhaps you only dream of vacations to Hawaii and designer clothes to hide your lumps and bumps. Your home may be filled with worn and spotted upholstery with rugs to match, and your car may be a Volkswagen bus. But if you are a mother in a home where *you* pray, and you teach your children to pray, you can count yourself wealthy and among the truly affluent!

A young mother in my stake recently died, leaving a family, the youngest member of which was ten years old. She was in her own home the last two weeks of her life, and in those last sacred days, it was my privilege to

talk to her. Do you know of what she spoke? Of her concern for her husband and children. She felt guilty because she was putting them through so much pain and anguish as she was dying. Her very last words were concern for their welfare, not for her own. She was dying of cancer and was in great pain, yet she did not want *them* to suffer. How ironic. How like an angel.

However, this young mother would be the first to admit she was no angel. She was a normal mother, impatient, sometimes angry, one who had regrets for nagging.

At her funeral, the stake president shared this young mother's feelings of being needed and of her importance to her family. She had told the stake president that if anyone at her funeral said she was needed beyond the veil more than she was needed here with her family, she would rise from her coffin and declare: "That is not true!"

Here was an angel mother (with a sense of humor) who had done the best she knew how, and her best was good enough. Despite what we mothers think and feel about ourselves, this is a good description of most mothers.

A mother is simply someone who does the best that she can with what she has to work with. Knowing that, you can have confidence in yourself and shed your inappropriate guilt. Would the Lord condemn you for your failure to do what you didn't know how to do, or didn't understand, or didn't have the strength to do? Never!

Mothers, be comforted if you are putting forth your best efforts. Be at peace in your minds and in your hearts. In the sight of the Lord, your best is good enough. What else matters?